GO TURBO

EXTREME SPORTS

KATE SCARBOROUGH

EDGE
FRANKLIN WATTS
LONDON·SYDNEY

First published in 2009 by
Franklin Watts
338 Euston Road
London NW1 3BH

Franklin Watts Australia
Level 17/207 Kent Street
Sydney NSW 2000

Series editor: Adrian Cole
Art director: Jonathan Hair
Design: Blue Paw Design
Picture research: Sophie Hartley
Consultants: Fiona M. Collins and Philippa Hunt,
Roehampton University

A CIP catalogue record for this book is available from the British Library.

ISBN: 978 0 7496 8664 2

Dewey Classification: 796.04' 6

Acknowledgements:
© Fabrice Coffrini/EPA/Corbis: 34. © Duomo/Corbis: 11. © Jeff Flindt/NewSport/Corbis: 29. © Albert Gea/Reuters/Corbis: 20. Stephen
Alvarez/National Geographic/Getty Images: 16. John & Eliza Forder/Stone/Getty Images: 17. © iStockphoto.com/Rob Broek: 7b. ©
iStockphoto.com/Eric Foltz: Cover & 18-19. © iStockphoto.com/David Livingston: 6. © iStockphoto.com/Hector Mandel: 36b. ©
iStockphoto.com/Sean McDermid: 6-7. © iStockphoto.com/Jeff McDonald: 36t. © iStockphoto.com/Christophe Michot: 37b. ©
iStockphoto.com/Steven Robertson: 9 & 38. © iStockphoto.com/Dejan Sarman: 35. © iStockphoto.com/Andreas Weber: 38-39. ©
iStockphoto.com/Ihsan Yildizli: 7t. Guillermo Arias/AP/PA Photos: 14. Greg Baker/AP/PA Photos: 10. Deutsche Press-Agentur/DPA/PA
Photos: 18. Kevin Novak/ABACA USA/PA Photos: 13. © Shutterstock.com: 37t. © Shutterstock.com/Bruno Ismael da Silva Alves: 40. ©
Shutterstock.com/Evron: 32. © Shutterstock.com/Josue Adib Cervantes Garcia: 14-15. © Shutterstock.com/Jarvis Gray: 28. ©
Shutterstock.com/Charles Knox: 8. © Shutterstock.com/Eric Limon: 21. © Shutterstock.com/Jason Merideth: 33. © Shutterstock.com/Fesus
Robert: 41. © Shutterstock.com/Ali Mazraie Shadi: Endpapers. © Shutterstock.com/Dorian C. Shy: 12. © Shutterstock.com/Clive Watkins:
30. © Shutterstock.com/Alexey Zarubin: 31

Printed in China

Franklin Watts is a division of Hachette Children's Books,
an Hachette UK company.
www.hachette.co.uk

Contents

Words that are highlighted can be found in the glossary.

What is an extreme sport?

Extreme **sports are tough, fast and exciting. Most are not team games and have few rules. Many extreme sports need special equipment.**

Snowboarding

Many younger people take part in extreme sports for the thrills. People usually start learning when they are young. As they get older the sports become more difficult and more dangerous, for example, the jumps in snowboarding get bigger.

White-water rafting

Paragliding

Mountaineering

 Look back at the contents page – which sport would you most like to try?

Skateboarding

Skateboarders are often called skaters or shredders. They perform tricks to show off their skills.

The most important trick is the ollie (see below). This trick is a jump from flat ground with the skateboard. From the ollie, the kickflip and heelflip were also created.

GT Record

The highest recorded ollie from flat ground is 113 centimetres (cm). It was performed by Danny Wainwright from Great Britain at the Reese Forbes Ollie Challenge in 2000.

? Watch Danny Wainwright perform a kickflip or heelflip at the website on the right. Which words can you think of to describe how he does the tricks?

Go Turbo Tricks

- Many skateboard tricks were invented in the 1970s and 1980s.
- Simple tricks include riding on the back two wheels, called a wheelie.
- Did you know that jumping off a skateboard, over an object, and landing on the skateboard again, is called a hippie jump?

Skaters perform tricks in skateparks with ramps.

ONLINE//:

http://www.youtube.com
Search 'Danny Wainwright' and select and watch him preparing for his world-record attempt – and then making it!

BMX

BMX bikes are designed to race and do tricks. They are small bikes and usually have 20-inch wheels.

When they race, BMX riders speed along dirt tracks. When they perform tricks they ride on streets, dirt ramps and on huge ramps called **verts**. Performing tricks is called freestyle.

BMX racing entered the Olympics for the first time at Beijing in 2008.

The most extreme BMX tricks are performed on the **halfpipe**, such as the one below. By picking up speed, riders can backflip and do 360 degree spins.

GT Record

In 2001, Dave Mirra performed a world-record 5.8 metre (m) jump from a 5.4m vert ramp.

ONLINE//:

http://bmx-stunts.freeonlinegames.com
This site has a cool little game to play, where you control a character and perform BMX tricks. Try it and compare scores with your friends.

Freestyle motocross

In freestyle motocross (or FMX), riders perform motorbike jumps and tricks, rather than race each other. There are two types of FMX competition: big air and freestyle.

In big air, riders like the one above get three jumps from a ramp. In freestyle, riders perform two routines, lasting between 90 seconds and 14 minutes.

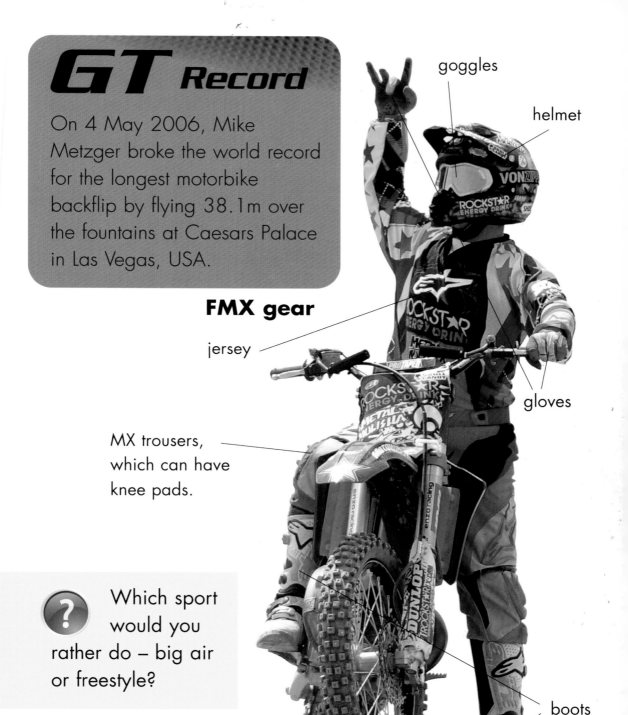

GT Record

On 4 May 2006, Mike Metzger broke the world record for the longest motorbike backflip by flying 38.1m over the fountains at Caesars Palace in Las Vegas, USA.

FMX gear

goggles

helmet

jersey

gloves

MX trousers, which can have knee pads.

boots

? Which sport would you rather do – big air or freestyle?

ONLINE//:

www.ifmxf.com/gallerys_2008.jsp
Go to the website of International Freestyle Motocross for fantastic photos and videos of FMX big air and freestyle.

Rallying

In rally racing, drivers and co-drivers race from point to point to see who is the fastest. They race on roads and tracks. Track conditions can include gravel, dirt and sometimes snow.

GT Top Fact

Rally cars have top speeds of up to 225**kph**, but usually travel slower than this because of the track conditions.

Rally drivers use pacenotes. These are detailed descriptions of the road or track. The co-driver reads the pacenotes out to the driver. He can then prepare for jumps or corners before they happen.

The biggest racing event is the World Rally Championship (WRC). One of the most famous rally races is the Monte Carlo Rally, which started in 1911.

Rally races are tough events and the cars have to be strong with powerful engines.

ONLINE//:

www.wrc.com
Visit the home of the FIA World Rally Championship to find out about the teams, and also watch videos showing the tough track conditions.

Caving

Cavers explore deep underground cave systems. They climb, crawl, dig, dive and swim through underground passages.

All cavers explore in teams for safety. They use special gear including hard hats, ropes, lights and tough boots. Many caves have water in them, so cavers often wear waterproof clothing.

GT Record

The longest-ever cave dive recorded was completed in Florida, USA in December 2007. Jarrod Jablonski and Casey McKinlay swam through 11.25 kilometres (km) of underground freshwater caves. The journey took six hours.

GT Top Fact

In 1991, caver Emily Davis Mobley broke her leg and became trapped underground in New Mexico, USA. More than 70 people worked over four days to bring her to the surface. This was the deepest and most remote cave rescue in US history.

Steep holes to climb down are called pitches (above), and narrow passageways are known as squeezes. **?** Can you think what the dangers might be when caving?

ONLINE//:

www.goodearthgraphics.com/virtcave
Explore different kinds of caves from the safety of your seat! Check out the fantastic illustrations of different cave systems.

Mountaineering

Mountaineers climb up cliffs and mountains over rock, snow and ice – just for thrills! Some people aim to conquer the mountain by reaching the top. Other people just want to practise their climbing skills.

GT Record

The first to conquer Mount Everest were Sir Edmund Hillary (right) and Sherpa Tensing in 1953.

? What do you think it was like for them up on the mountain?

The three highest mountains in the world are Mount Everest (8,848m), K2 (8,611m) and Kangchenjunga (8,586m). They are all in the Himalayas.

Mountaineers climb in groups. Sometimes, if the mountain is very high, they camp on its steep slopes. On the largest mountains there is a **base camp**, where there is always a supply team. Up on the mountain, climbers use tents or dig into the snow to make snow caves.

Climbing gear

rope

carabiner

harness

chalk bag

rubber climbing shoes

Snowboarding

Snowboarders, or 'shredders', speed down snowy slopes with both feet attached to a single board. Some snowboarders compete in downhill races. They twist past poles in a set course. This is called a slalom race.

GT Top Fact

In the Super G (Super Giant slalom), the fastest snowboarding race, riders can travel as fast as 72kph.

This Super G rider leans into a sharp turn.

Some snowboarders perform tricks to impress judges and win points. Snowboarders fly off icy ramps to do high jumps, or go from side to side performing tricks in a halfpipe.

? Can you make up a new snowboarding word? Real ones include 'fakie' (riding backwards) and 'steezy' (style with ease).

ONLINE//:

www.abc-of-snowboarding.com
Visit this website for everything you want to know about snowboarding, including more tricks and a beginners' guide.

Halfpipe Dream

Written by Leon Read   Illustrated by Kevin Hopgood

It's minus 15°C out here, but I can't feel the cold. I'm watching the giant video screen as Lucy Holden completes her final halfpipe run. She's totally killed it, very technical, great amplitude. Thing is, I'm not really watching. I'm thinking about Mum, Dad and Jen. Jen was my older brother, and a great shredder. But six years ago there was an accident, back home in the mountains, and now he's gone. He gave me my dream – to be just like him. And now I'm here at the Winter Olympics.

I put those thoughts on hold. Lucy Holden is on the screen again. She blows hot breath on her finger so in the cold air it looks like a smoking gun – as if she's won already! We've been going at each other all season, she's beaten me every time. I've made some big runs though.

Lucy's score comes up. Cameras flash in the dark. Horns and whistles blare out. She's in first place – gold medal position. She's knocked me down to second place again. There's only one more shredder to make a run. Me!

The conditions are perfect tonight. It hasn't snowed since yesterday and the pipe – almost 150 metres long – is smooth and silky. Its near-vertical ice walls are almost seven metres high.

I'm at the top, my snowboard on my boots. Energy rushing through me. I fix my headphones and the music crashes into my ears. Then I drop down, time to dial-in my moves. I get height off the first wall, pull a cute mute air, then drop back with speed into a backside 540. The landing is so good I can't help smiling.

Then I link to a cab 720 with a melon grab – almost over run it – but something lands me smoothly. I'm popping so much height off the wall, like I'm flying. Riding with an angel on my shoulder.

The music speeds me into a solid frontside 900, linking to a backside 360, both with stylish grabs. Again I almost hold them too long – but it only makes them look better. I power up the wall and flip into a crippler.
Now the crowd goes WOW!

Before I know it I've finished my run. People are cheering all around. But I'm not sure if it was enough.

My score comes up. It's 96.8! I'm top of the table – the gold-medal winner – Olympic champion. My face is up on the video screen, and I'm smiling.

Next thing I know, I'm standing on the winners' platform wearing a heavy gold medal. Then they play the national anthem. I can't help crying. Everyone thinks it's because I've won. But all I can think about is Jen – how he would have loved this. Well, this is for you brother.

GT Snowboarding words

Amplitude – trick height

Backside / Frontside – heel edge / toe edge

Cab – short for Caballerial, a trick that begins riding backwards and lands riding forwards

Crippler – 180 degree flip

Melon grab – the front hand grabs the heel edge between the feet, push the front leg straight

Mute – the front hand grabs the toe edge near the toes

Surfing

Surfers catch waves that push them towards the shore. Once the waves start to push the boards forward the surfers leap to their feet. Falling from a board while surfing is called a wipeout.

Surfers use different types of board. These include short 'body boards' (above) and longer 'cruisers' (right).

Go Turbo Tricks

'Hanging ten' is when the surfer has both feet at the front of the board with ten toes hanging over its edge.

GT Record

Experienced surfers hunt for bigger and bigger waves. Waimea Bay in Hawaii, below, has some of the highest waves in the world at 9 to 15m high.

ONLINE//:

www.markfennell.com/flash/wipeout
Try this quick online game – watch out for the sharks! How often do you wipeout?

Kitesurfing

Kitesurfing is one of the fastest growing extreme sports. Kitesurfers use the power of the wind in their kites to pull them over the waves, rather than the power of the sea.

Kitesurfers have to be skilled surfers and kite flyers. They learn and develop kite skills on land before heading out to sea.

Kitesurfers can perform more tricks than surfers. They leap into the air. Each jump has a name, such as kickflip, jibe or aerial.

GT Top Fact

Kitesurfing boards are about 1.4m long with foot straps and an ankle leash. The leash stops the kitesurfer from losing the board.

GT Record

The longest a kitesurfer has ever ridden to date is 225km without stopping. This record is held by Kirsty Jones from Wales, UK.

ONLINE//:

http://kitesurfingschool.org
Log on to this crazy kitesurfing site for guides to kitesurfing techniques and amazing kitesurfing photographs.

White-water rafting

Rafting started when people built flat platforms to carry goods downstream. **Today rafts can take people down dangerous stretches of water – just for fun!**

Every other year the rafting world championships are held. Teams and individuals compete in races and in specially designed courses called slaloms.

The different parts of a river are classed from 1 to 6 depending on how dangerous they are. Level 6 is impossible to take a raft down. People would only survive through luck and not skill.

? Rafters wear jackets to keep them afloat. Why do they wear hard hats?

GT Record

In June 2006, Captain Chris Reeder and his team set a new record for the longest distance paddled in a day. They rafted 194.21 river miles (312.55km) in 24 hours along rivers in Colorado, USA.

ONLINE//:

http://www.intraftfed.com/gallery/videos.html
Check out the great videos and images of rafting races on the website of the International Rafting Federation.

Free diving

Free divers do not use breathing equipment under water. They hold their breath for long periods of time.

Some divers hold their breath in a swimming pool. Others hold their breath and dive down into the sea as far as they can go.

Just holding your breath without moving is called static **apnea**. Diving without air is often called competitive apnea. Divers can use big fins on their feet.

GT Record

Tom Sietas from Germany held his breath under water for 10 minutes 12 seconds during a static apnea competition.

Free divers have to be very fit. They learn how to hold their breath for long periods of time. One way of training is to hold a breath and then walk as far as possible before taking another breath. The best free divers can walk up to 400m without needing to breathe.

 How far can you walk on one breath?

This free diver is using a fin to help swim back to the surface.

Skydiving

Skydivers fall towards the ground at speeds of up to 190kph. They jump from an aeroplane at around 4,000m, only releasing their parachutes at around 900m.

The parachutes have controls that allow skydivers to move through the air in certain directions. The landing site they aim for is called the dropzone.

Wingsuit divers fall at speeds of around 95kph. This slower speed allows them to travel greater distances than skydivers across the sky.

GT Record

A Swiss daredevil, Ueli 'Sputnik' Gegenschatz, set a record for the longest flight with a wingsuit on a 17.6km journey over Ireland.

Paragliding and hang gliding

Both these sports involve jumping off the side of a hill or mountain. Hang gliders lie in a harness and hold an arrow-shaped wing. Paragliders are attached to a fabric wing and sit upright in a harness.

Both hang gliders (below) and paragliders (right) use a variometer, which tells them whether they are rising or falling in the air. They also have a radio and **GPS (global positioning system)**.

GT Record

Hang gliders speed: 30–145kph.
Paragliders speed: 20–60kph.

GT *Top Fact*

On 14 February 2007, a German paraglider was sucked into a large cloud. She accidently flew to a height of 9,946m before she passed out through lack of **oxygen**. She landed almost three-and-a-half hours later, alive and covered in ice.

ONLINE//:

http://video.google.com/
Type 'paraglider crash' into the search box for a look at the scary side of paragliding.

Air racing

Small aircraft racing started back in 1909, just six years after the Wright brothers **invented the first powered aeroplane. Today air racing is the fastest motorsport in the world.**

Air-racing planes twist and turn quickly.

In Red Bull racing, planes fly between air-filled poles on a set course. The pilots reach speeds of 370kph while resisting forces of up to 10gs (G-force).

GT Top Fact

G-force is the pressure forced on you when you travel at speed.

- On a rollercoaster ride you may feel 2gs.
- Formula 1 racing drivers feel 5gs on fast corners.
- Racing pilots feel 10gs on fast, steep climbs and turns — it is like having 100kg on top of you!

Air races take place every year in Reno, Nevada, USA. All types of plane compete, from light aircraft to jet planes.

ONLINE//:

www.redbullairrace.com For fantastic facts on Red Bull races.
www.airrace.org Website of the National Air Races.

Fast facts

Tony Hawk landed the first-ever 900 (two-and-a-half, mid-air rotations) on a skateboard at the 1999 X Games in San Francisco.

BMX rider Mat Hoffman jumped his bike off a 1066m cliff with a parachute.

Caleb Wyatt landed the first ever backflip on a motocross bike.

The world's largest outdoor skatepark is the Millennium Skate Park in Calgary, Canada.

Danny Way set the record for the biggest air when he flew 19.8m in the air after dropping down a 15m roll-in at the King of Skate competition in 2002.

In 1997, German stuntman Jochen Schweizer pulled off the world's longest bungee jump. Schweizer plunged more than 1,012m from a helicopter.

Answers

These are suggestions to questions in this book. You may find that you have other answers. Talk about them with your friends. They may have other answers too.

Pages 7, 13, 21, 35: The answers to these questions will depend on your own choices.

Page 8: Some comments on the website might help you.

Page 17: The dangers of caving include cavers getting too cold, drowning in sudden floods, falling down cave drops, being trapped in collapsed tunnels, being hit by falling rocks and getting lost.

Page 18: As Edmund Hillary and Sherpa Tensing headed for the summit they were tired after a night spent trying to sleep in the bitter cold on the slopes. They had oxygen equipment to help them breathe. To read more go to: *imagingeverest.rgs.org/Concepts/Imaging_Everest/-75.html*

Page 33: Rafters wear hard hats to protect their heads from rocks in the water. If the raft capsizes, the rafters can be swept underwater and washed against the rocks.

More websites

The personal website of Danny Way, one of the best skateboarders on the planet. Includes photos, videos and skateboarding news:

http://dannyway.com

The website for the US Extreme sport TV channel – with loads of videos and news:

http://expn.go.com/ expn/index

One of the best known professional skateboarders, Tony Hawk, has a whole website dedicated to him:

http://www.tonyhawk. com

The website of Tanya Streeter, world-record free diver:

http://www.redefineyo urlimits.com

Watch videos of others trying out BMX tricks and learning how to do them, as well as watching the expert:

www.davemirra.com

For all mountaineering guidance and information try the British Mountaineering Council:

www.thebmc.co.uk

Skating and snowboarding photos, videos and news on a range of extreme sports:

www.extreme.com/ ExtremeSports

Funny, mad and bad videos of people playing and doing extreme sports – or at least trying:

www.extremesportclips. com

Glossary

Apnea – a technical word for someone who stops breathing for more than 10–15 seconds.

Base camp – the place on the lowest slopes of a mountain where mountaineers set up a camp. It provides shelter for a support team and storage for equipment.

Carabiner – a snap-link hoop used to connect ropes.

Chalk bag – used to hold a climber's chalk. They use it to stop their hands slipping.

Conquer – to beat or win over someone or something.

Downstream – rivers flow down from their source to the sea. Anything that is down from the source is called downstream.

Extreme – being of a high level of difficulty or intensity, or being more than what is normal.

Global positioning system – a satellite system that allows people to find their position anywhere on Earth.

Halfpipe – a structure shaped like a pipe cut in half used in skateboarding, BMX, snowboarding or motocross to perform tricks and jumps.

Kph – short for kilometres per hour, a measurement of distance travelled and the time taken.

Oxygen – the gas in the air which we breathe to stay alive.

Verts – short for vertical, the section of the halfpipe or a separate structure which slopes straight up into the air.

Wingsuit – a specially designed suit used by skydivers. The suit has extra flaps under the arms and between the legs which act like wings. These wings help skydivers to stay in the air for longer, but they still have a parachute.

Wright brothers – two American brothers, Orville and Wilbur, who were the first to design an aircraft that flew with an engine in 1903.

Index